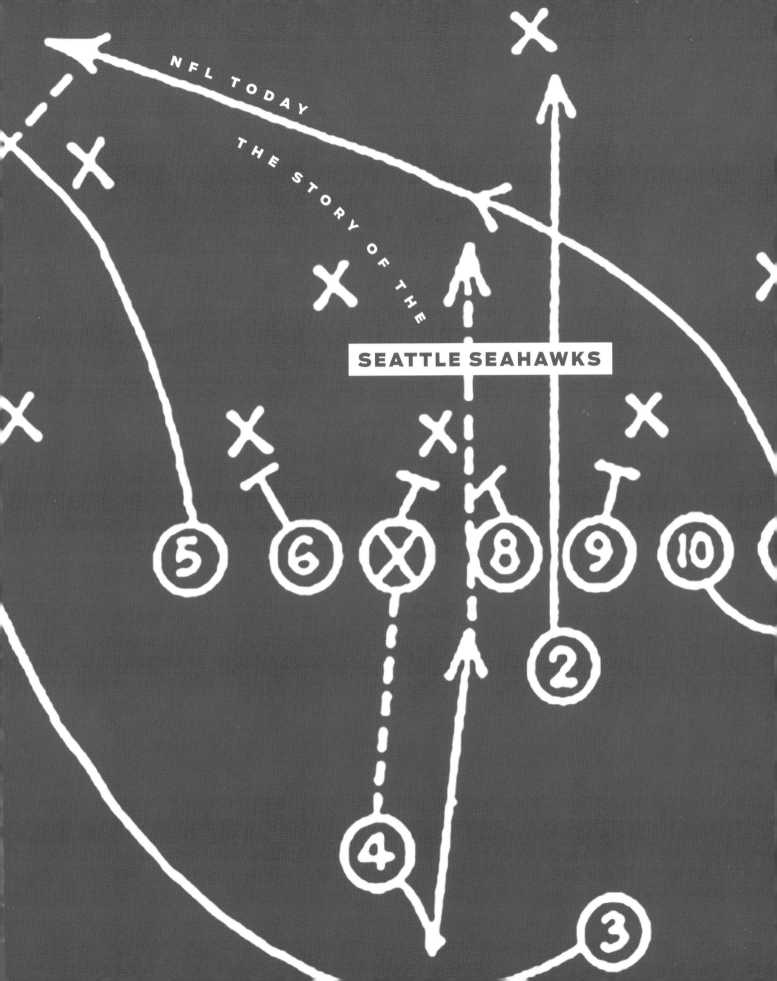

NFL TODAY

THE STORY OF THE

SEATTLE SEAHAWKS

NFL TODAY

THE STORY OF THE SEATTLE SEAHAWKS

JIM WHITING

CREATIVE EDUCATION

PUBLISHED BY CREATIVE EDUCATION
P.O. BOX 227, MANKATO, MINNESOTA 56002
CREATIVE EDUCATION IS AN IMPRINT OF THE CREATIVE COMPANY
WWW.THECREATIVECOMPANY.US

DESIGN AND PRODUCTION BY BLUE DESIGN
ART DIRECTION BY RITA MARSHALL
PRINTED IN THE UNITED STATES OF AMERICA

PHOTOGRAPHS BY AP IMAGES (AP PHOTO/NFL
PHOTOS), CORBIS (BETTMANN, JOSE FUSTE RAGA,
TROY WAYRYNEN/COLUMBIAN/NEWS SPORT),
CORKY TREWIN (PETE GROSS), GETTY IMAGES
(JAY BIGGERSTAFF/TUSP, JONATHAN DANIEL,
MIGUEL A. ELLIOTT, JONATHAN FERREY, GEORGE
GOJKOVICH, STEVE GRAYSON/NFL, OTTO GREULE JR.,
DREW HALLOWELL, TOM HAUCK, JED JACOBSOHN,
JED JACOBSOHN/ALLSPORT, CRAIG JONES, BOB
LEVERONE/SPORTING NEWS, NFL, CHRISTIAN
PETERSEN, MIKE POWELL, RICK STEWART, DAMIAN
STROHMEYER, KEVIN TERRELL/NFL, CORKY CHARLES
TREWIN, GREG TROTT/NFL, MAXX WOLFSON)

LIBRARY OF CONGRESS CATALOGING-IN-PUBLICATION DATA
WHITING, JIM.
THE STORY OF THE SEATTLE SEAHAWKS / BY JIM WHITING.
P. CM. — (NFL TODAY)
INCLUDES INDEX.
SUMMARY: THE HISTORY OF THE NATIONAL FOOTBALL LEAGUE'S
SEATTLE SEAHAWKS, SURVEYING THE FRANCHISE'S BIGGEST
STARS AND MOST MEMORABLE MOMENTS FROM ITS INAUGURAL
SEASON IN 1976 TO TODAY.
ISBN 978-1-60818-320-3
1. SEATTLE SEAHAWKS (FOOTBALL TEAM)—HISTORY—JUVENILE
LITERATURE. I. TITLE.

GV956.S4W55 2013
796.332'6409797772—DC23   2012033818

FIRST EDITION
9 8 7 6 5 4 3 2 1

COVER: QUARTERBACK RUSSELL WILSON
PAGE 2: WIDE RECEIVER BEN OBOMANU
PAGES 4–5: CENTURYLINK FIELD
PAGE 6: 2007 SEATTLE SEAHAWKS

TABLE OF CONTENTS

Football in the Northwest

Ask people in other parts of the United States what they know about Seattle—tucked away in the Pacific Northwest—and their answer is likely to be, "It rains there a lot." Actually, that's not entirely true. Seattle's annual rainfall is about 38 inches a year. That ranks it number 44 among major cities in the U.S. Cities such as Philadelphia (41 inches), New York (43), Boston (44), Miami (58), and New Orleans (60) all get more wet stuff than Seattle, a metropolis of more than 600,000 people also known for grunge bands, Starbucks Coffee, and "Microsoft Millionaires"—employees of the world's largest software company who were early hires and became enormously wealthy as the company's stock price soared.

This misconception of Seattle may be one reason it took the National Football League (NFL) so long to come calling. The league finally granted Seattle a franchise in June

TACKLE NORM EVANS FINISHED HIS CAREER AS AN INAUGURAL MEMBER OF THE SEAHAWKS

Jim Zorn

QUARTERBACK / SEAHAWKS SEASONS: 1976–84 / HEIGHT: 6-FOOT-2 / WEIGHT: 200 POUNDS

Jim Zorn was the perfect fit as the Seattle Seahawks' first quarterback. Like the new team, Zorn was young, energetic, and eager to improve. And although he immediately made his mark as a rookie, when he earned team Most Valuable Player (MVP) and conference Offensive Rookie of the Year honors, he and the Seahawks collectively improved during his tenure with the team. By 1979, he had almost doubled his touchdown production and increased his passing totals by about 1,000 yards. His arm was amazingly accurate, and his feet were frighteningly quick; when he wasn't passing the football, he often ran. Most often, however, Zorn was directing the ball into the hands of receiver Steve Largent, the young quarterback's favorite downfield target. By the time Zorn left Seattle, he had amassed a total of 20,122 passing yards and 107 touchdown passes. "I'm just happy to be a Seahawk as long as I was," Zorn said. "I wish it would have been longer." After retiring, he became a college and professional coach. In 2008, he was voted into the State of Washington Sports Hall of Fame.

AFTER A BANNER 1984 SEASON, DAVE BROWN ATTENDED HIS ONLY PRO BOWL

1974, a month and a half after doing the same thing for Tampa Bay, Florida. Seattle's relative isolation proved to be a boon in terms of fan support. If the Dallas Cowboys are "America's Team," Seattle became the "Northwest's Team," attracting fans from Oregon, Idaho, Montana, Canada, and Alaska in addition to Washington state.

The first order of business in getting the Seattle franchise up and running was naming it. The owners turned to the fans for suggestions. More than 20,000 responded, offering 1,741 possibilities, from *A* (Aleuts and Asparagus) to *Z* (Zodiacs). The winning choice was Seahawks, which appeared on 151 ballots. The namesake is a large, powerful bird of prey that frequents Northwest coastal areas.

he team's first coach, Jack Patera, also frequented the Northwest coast. He grew up in Portland, Oregon, and played defensive tackle at the University of Oregon before turning to coaching. The Seahawks job represented his first head coaching opportunity. Patera's initial Seahawks team was made up primarily of veteran castoffs nearing the end of their careers. A few, such as cornerback Dave Brown—called the "Original Seahawk" because he would stay with the team until 1986—made significant contributions.

Seattle's veterans were complemented by young, unproven talents plucked from the NFL Draft. One was wide receiver Steve Raible, who would play for six years and later become the club's play-by-play announcer in 2004. The Seahawks also signed quarterback Jim Zorn, who was so lightly regarded that he manned a jackhammer to help build the team's headquarters and worked part-time in the team's

"I'm just happy to be a Seahawk."

JIM ZORN

public relations department because he had so little money when he came to Seattle. Then, just before the season began, the Seahawks got a huge break. They traded a future eighth-round draft pick to the Houston Oilers for wide receiver Steve Largent, who would become one of the NFL's all-time greatest pass-catchers (amassing 819 receptions and 100 touchdowns over his career).

Zorn became an instant hero in the team's first game of the 1976 season by leading a furious rally that nearly overcame the St. Louis Cardinals in a 30–24 defeat, throwing a pair of touchdown passes and scoring a touchdown himself. "That [Seattle's rally] wasn't supposed to happen," St. Louis coach Don Coryell told reporters. "They were better prepared than we expected."

It took a while for this preparation to bear fruit, as the Seahawks dropped their next four games to open the season 0–5. Tampa Bay likewise started 0–5. The two expansion teams then met in an ugly game that included 35 penalties. Finally, the Seahawks blocked a game-tying field goal with 42 seconds left to notch a 13–10 victory—Seattle's first and one of only two the team would enjoy all year. Nevertheless, optimism ran high. Fans sensed the chemistry building among the Seahawks' young players, especially between Zorn and Largent. Zorn threw for almost 2,600 yards and earned NFL Offensive Rookie of the Year honors.

The Seahawks quickly climbed the standings in the American Football Conference (AFC) West Division in the following seasons. Seattle jumped to 5–9 in 1977, then posted back-to-back 9–7 records in 1978 and 1979. A notable addition during this time was linebacker Keith Butler, who would become the second-leading tackler in team history. Patera's creative play-calling made national news after Seattle's first *Monday Night Football* appearance in October 1979. The Seahawks came back from a 14–0 deficit to beat the Atlanta Falcons 31–28, thanks in part to a fake field goal pass from Zorn to kicker Efren Herrera. Legendary broadcaster Howard Cosell proclaimed, "The Seahawks are giving the nation a lesson in entertaining football!"

Things got tougher in 1980. After defeating the New York Jets 27–17 in mid-October, the Seahawks went winless for the rest of the season and dropped to 4–12, finishing last in the AFC West. Despite the additions of safety Kenny Easley and running back Theotis Brown, the 1981 Seahawks struggled

The Voice Is Stilled

From the beginning, Pete Gross was the Seahawks' radio voice, broadcasting every game with enthusiasm and a deep knowledge of the sport. So it was with considerable dismay that Seattle players and fans learned in 1988 that Gross had kidney cancer. He battled the ravages of the disease with courage and optimism, but seven games into the 1992 season, he had to give up the microphone. In late November, the Seahawks honored Gross with a ceremony before a *Monday Night Football* game against Miami by inducting him into the team's Ring of Honor. Riding an eight-game losing streak, the team rallied to tie the game in the final minute, then kicked a field goal to win 16–13 in overtime. Two days later, Gross died. "One of the most beloved people to have ever been associated with the Seahawks franchise, fans will never forget his numerous 'touchdown Seahawks' calls," said the State of Washington Sports Hall of Fame. During his treatment, Gross realized that Seattle lacked a place where out-of-town cancer patients could stay. He joined with community leaders to create the Pete Gross House, a 70-unit facility that provides a lasting legacy.

PETE GROSS MISSED ONLY 5 GAMES (ALL IN 1992) IN 17 YEARS OF ANNOUNCING

KENNY EASLEY WAS NAMED AP DEFENSIVE PLAYER OF THE YEAR IN 1984

from the start. After being crushed 32–0 by the New York Giants, the Seahawks held a miserable 1–6 record. "Congratulations," a grumpy Coach Patera told them. "You're now the worst team in the National Football League. I'll see you tomorrow."

The next day, Patera put his players through a series of rigorous drills in full pads and was rewarded with a 19–3 victory the following week. But the Seahawks still finished in the division cellar with a 6–10 record. The next season began with two straight losses before a players' strike occurred in mid-September. By the time the NFL resumed play in late November, Patera had been fired, and the Seahawks finished the shortened season 4–5. One bright spot was the addition of defensive tackle Joe Nash, who would play in more games (218) than any other Seahawks player.

Steve Largent

WIDE RECEIVER / SEAHAWKS SEASONS: 1976–89 / HEIGHT: 5-FOOT-11 / WEIGHT: 187 POUNDS

Steve Largent was selected by Houston in the fourth round of the 1976 NFL Draft. After four disappointing preseason games, he was traded to Seattle, where he became one of the premier receivers in the game. Exceptionally sure-handed, Largent became quarterback Jim Zorn's go-to guy almost immediately and held the same distinction through his entire career. He was the first Seahawks player selected to play in the Pro Bowl, which he did seven times, and the first retired player named to the team's Ring of Honor, which recognizes outstanding team players. When he retired in 1989, Largent held NFL records for career receptions (819), career receiving yards (13,089) and career touchdown receptions (100). He still holds franchise records for both single-season and career receiving yards, and is one of only two Seahawks players (along with Cortez Kennedy) in the Pro Football Hall of Fame. "It might have been the dumbest move I've ever made," former Oilers coach Bum Phillips said of his trading Largent. After his football days were over, Largent went on to serve four terms (eight years) in the U.S. House of Representatives as a representative from his home state of Oklahoma.

Bring on the Noise

The Seattle Seahawks may have the greatest home-field advantage in all of football. CenturyLink Field (formerly Qwest Field), where the team has played since 2002, is widely considered the loudest stadium in the NFL. That's no accident: team owner and Microsoft cofounder Paul Allen, who paid $160 million of the $460 million it cost to build CenturyLink Field out of his own pocket, asked the architects to direct as much of the crowd noise as possible onto the field. He also approved the use of metal bleachers, which reverberate loudly when fans start stomping. The enthusiastic fans sometimes make so much noise when cheering that opposing teams struggle to hear the quarterback call the play, which can often result in false-start penalties. In one 2005 game, the New York Giants received 11 false-start penalties and ended up losing to the Seahawks 24–21 in overtime. "That stuff matters," Seattle quarterback Matt Hasselbeck said after the game. "It matters in a big, big way. If that game was at Giants Stadium, we wouldn't have won it, I know that."

IN 2012, LEAGUE-WIDE RULE CHANGES ABOUT STADIUM NOISE HELPED "CLINK" GET ROWDIER

The Coach Knox Era

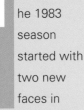

The 1983 season started with two new faces in Seattle: coach Chuck Knox, who had previously led both the Los Angeles Rams and the Buffalo Bills to the playoffs, and running back Curt Warner, who had led Penn State University to the national college championship the year before. Warner was poised to play a prominent role in Knox's new offensive scheme.

Zorn, however, would not. Injuries hobbled him in 1982 and hurt his performance in 1983. When a pass intended for Warner fell to the ground three feet away from the running back just before halftime in Week 8, Zorn could tell by his coach's reaction that it was over. The second half started with Dave Krieg under center. "I just had a sense that they were waiting for me to do something so they could put Dave in there," Zorn said later. "It was a lot more difficult being demoted

CURT WARNER'S 14 TOUCHDOWNS WAS THE THIRD-BEST TOTAL IN THE NFL IN 1983

Chuck Knox

COACH / SEAHAWKS SEASONS: 1983–91

By the time Chuck Knox signed on as the head coach of the Seattle Seahawks in 1983, he had already been on NFL sidelines for more than 20 years and had served as head coach of the Los Angeles (now St. Louis) Rams and the Buffalo Bills for the previous 10. He inherited a veteran-heavy Seahawks team that had posted winning records only twice and had not yet played in a postseason game. When he came to Seattle, Knox laid down a whole new set of rules for the players—and immediately found success. In his first season with the Seahawks, the no-nonsense coach led Seattle to a 9–7 record and took the team within one game of the Super Bowl. Knox, who stayed in Seattle for nine seasons, returned to the playoffs three more times during his tenure with the team. He compiled an 80–63 record with the Seahawks and a 186–147–1 record as a professional coach. In 2005, Knox was inducted into the Seahawks' Ring of Honor, joining the company of seven of his former players.

"When it happened, the place went dead silent."

PAUL MOYER ON CURT WARNER'S INJURY IN 1984

than being cut." Krieg threw two touchdowns in the second half and earned the starting job. With the help of Warner, who ran for 1,449 yards, and kicker Norm Johnson, who tallied 103 points, Krieg led the Seahawks to a 9–7 record and their first trip to the playoffs.

 rieg delivered a near-perfect performance in the postseason's first round, completing 12 of 13 passes and tossing 3 touchdowns as the Seahawks crushed the Denver Broncos 31–7. Few people thought he could pull off the same magic against the Miami Dolphins the next week. When Seattle fell behind by three points with less than four minutes remaining in the fourth quarter, it didn't look good. Then Krieg connected with Largent twice to set up a Warner touchdown run for a 24–20 lead. A Johnson field goal sealed the thrilling 27–20 victory, which Largent called "one of the best games the Seahawks ever played." The team then traveled to Los Angeles to face the Raiders in the AFC Championship Game. Although the Seahawks lost that contest 30–14, they had proven themselves to be a force.

The 1984 season started with high hopes. But as the Seahawks routed the Cleveland Browns 33–0 in the season opener, Warner went down with a season-ending knee injury. "When it happened, the place went dead silent," safety Paul Moyer recalled. "Really quiet."

Surprisingly, losing Warner didn't prevent the Seahawks from posting a 12–4 record and then playing host to Los Angeles in a rematch with the Raiders in the opening round of the playoffs. This time, Seattle won and went on to face the Dolphins, who were in no mood for a repeat of the previous year. Miami crushed Seattle 31–10.

Seattle didn't return to the playoffs until 1987, aided by the arrival the previous year of fullback John L. Williams. But as the Seahawks built records of 8–8 in 1985 and 10–6 in 1986, they also beefed up their defense. Safety Eugene Robinson joined Easley in the defensive secondary, and defensive end Jacob Green anchored the line. With the impressive 1987 performance of the defense, and with Warner back in the lineup, Seattle returned to the postseason with a 9–6 record, only to lose a heartbreaker in overtime to Houston.

Cortez Kennedy

DEFENSIVE TACKLE / SEAHAWKS SEASONS: 1990–2000 / HEIGHT: 6-FOOT-3 / WEIGHT: 305 POUNDS

Cortez Kennedy almost missed his first season in Seattle. The Seahawks chose the All-American from the University of Miami with the third overall pick in the 1990 NFL Draft—but he didn't sign a contract until two days before the regular season started. That holdout resulted in a lackluster rookie campaign, with only 1 sack and 48 tackles, but it didn't hurt the rest of his career in Seattle. Kennedy, who played an entire decade with the Seahawks before retiring in 2000, "lived up to all our expectations," said coach Chuck Knox. The durable lineman played in 167 games, was named to 8 Pro Bowls, and was honored as an All-Pro 3 times. *Sports Illustrated* named him the best athlete to ever wear number 96. It came as a shock, therefore, when the Pro Football Hall of Fame passed him over for five years after he became eligible in 2007. "It's a shame he wasn't a first-ballot player because his talent is first-level talent," said New Orleans general manager Mickey Loomis. In 2012, the Hall of Fame finally voted him in. "I cried," Kennedy said. "It was so emotional to get that call to the Hall."

BRIAN BLADES MADE 2.5 RECEPTIONS PER GAME AS A ROOKIE IN 1988

In 1988, speedy wide receiver Brian Blades and powerful tight end Mike Tice helped the aging Largent lead the offense. The Seahawks went 9–7 to clinch their first AFC West championship and another trip to the postseason. Seattle couldn't get beyond the first round, though, losing to the Super Bowl–bound Cincinnati Bengals, 21–13.

hings then went downhill. Largent retired after the 1989 season. Warner left that same year to play with the Los Angeles Rams. Two years later, Krieg left town too, and Coach Knox—who had compiled an 80–63 record and taken the Seahawks to the playoffs four times during his nine-year tenure—was fired after a 7–9 showing in 1991. Knox remained thankful for his time with the Seahawks. "The fans here are the best fans of all the places I've been," he said. Knox left Seattle with the distinction of being the first head coach in NFL history to have won division titles with three different teams.

The only star left in Seattle when Tom Flores took over as head coach in 1992 was defensive tackle Cortez Kennedy, who led one of the best defenses in the league and was honored as the NFL's 1992

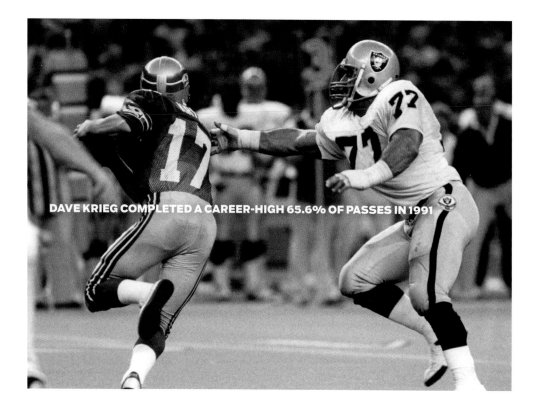

DAVE KRIEG COMPLETED A CAREER-HIGH 65.6% OF PASSES IN 1991

Defensive Player of the Year. Michael Sinclair was also emerging as a force at defensive end and would go on to be the league leader in sacks in 1998. But with a trio of inexperienced quarterbacks, the efforts of Kennedy, Sinclair, and their defensive teammates were wasted. The team's 140 total points in that miserable 2–14 season set an NFL record for the fewest points scored. "It was ugly," said Paul Moyer, who was now an assistant coach. "It was the most inept offense in the history of the NFL."

he silver lining to the Seahawks' slide was the opportunity to use the second pick of the 1993 NFL Draft to get Rick Mirer, a promising quarterback out of the University of Notre Dame. Mirer started every game in 1993, and his 2,833 passing yards (an NFL rookie record that broke the previous mark set by Zorn in 1976) and 12 touchdowns were causes for celebration in Seattle. With running back Chris Warren rushing for 1,072 yards, Seattle improved to 6–10.

The 12th Man

Twelve season-ticket holders from the Seahawks' inaugural season in 1976 gathered in the end zone of Seattle's Qwest Field on October 12, 2003. Together, they hoisted a blue flag emblazoned with the number 12 up a towering new flagpole. At every home game since then, that same flag in the southern end zone has been raised by a former Seahawks player or other local celebrity as part of a pregame ritual that honors the Seahawks' fans, who are so important that the team has often referred to them as the "12th man." Seattle has a history of thanking its faithful followers. In 1984, it became the first professional sports team to retire a jersey number in honor of its fans when it hung a number 12 jersey from the rafters of the Kingdome. And in 2005, after fan noise flustered the Giants in a critical game, contributing to a Seahawks win and a trip to the Super Bowl, head coach Mike Holmgren presented an honorary game ball to the crowd in appreciation of its support.

FOR ALL THEIR ANTICS, SEATTLE FANS TAKE THEIR 12TH MAN ROLE SERIOUSLY

RICK MIRER FELL PREY TO 138 SACKS IN ONLY 4 SEAHAWKS SEASONS

A Seahawks Surge

Unfortunately, that was the best Mirer could do. Even after successful college coach Dennis Erickson took over as head coach in 1995, the Seahawks finished a mediocre 8–8. After a 1–4 start in 1996, Mirer was benched. He was finally traded in 1997 and replaced by 40-year-old veteran Warren Moon, who promptly set team records for completions (313) and passing yards (3,678). "I wish I knew what it was [that keeps Moon going]," Coach Erickson said, "because I'd bottle it up and sell it out of my office."

Moon started for two seasons in Seattle. He and running back Ricky Watters, a free-agent signing prior to the 1998 season, brought the Seahawks to the brink of contention. With an 8–8 finish in 1998, the team missed the playoffs for the 10th straight season. Erickson was then fired, Moon was released, and the Seahawks started the last season of the century with a new coach and a new quarterback.

Seahawks owner Paul Allen had high hopes when he hired Mike Holmgren away from

RICKY WATTERS FLEW FOR NINE RUSHING TOUCHDOWNS IN 1998, HIS FIRST SEATTLE SEASON

Shaun Alexander

RUNNING BACK / SEAHAWKS SEASONS: 2000–07 / HEIGHT: 5-FOOT-11 / WEIGHT: 225 POUNDS

The 2005 season was a big one for Shaun Alexander. He broke records all season long, including the NFL mark for touchdowns scored in a season (28), and he ran away with the league rushing title with 1,880 yards. He also led the league in touchdowns, points scored, and Pro Bowl votes, and he beat out Indianapolis Colts star quarterback Peyton Manning for the NFL MVP award. But there were yet more honors in store for Alexander, who was selected by the Seahawks with the 19th pick of the 2000 NFL Draft after an award-winning college career at the University of Alabama. In December 2005, he made the cover of *Sports Illustrated*, becoming the first Seahawks player ever to earn the coveted spot on the weekly sports magazine. Unfortunately, after being rewarded with a stunning 8-year, $62-million contract, Alexander broke a bone in his foot in the third game of the 2006 season, limiting him to fewer than 900 yards in 10 games. After he gained only 716 yards and scored just 5 touchdowns in 2007, the Seahawks released him. He played briefly with Washington in 2008 before being released and ending his career.

WIDE RECEIVER KOREN ROBINSON DOVE FOR A SEAHAWKS BALL ALMOST 250 TIMES

Green Bay, where Holmgren had led the Packers out of a nine-year slump to Super Bowl appearances in 1996 and 1997. The Seahawks went 9–7 in 1999 and finally broke back into the playoffs. But when Seattle hosted Miami in the AFC Wild Card game—the last game played in the Kingdome, a multipurpose indoor stadium which was demolished to make way for a new outdoor facility—the Dolphins triumphed 20–17.

The hope of that season turned into frustration as Seattle's momentum then stalled, with the team posting 6–10 and 9–7 marks the next two years. Fans hoped that the opening of the new Seahawk Stadium (soon renamed Qwest Field) might provide a boost in 2002. The team also moved out of the AFC to become a part of the National Football Conference (NFC) West Division. But that season's campaign ended with a 7–9 record, and the Seahawks watched the playoffs from home for the third straight time.

Staying at home was not an option in 2003. That year, Matt Hasselbeck, who had played for Holmgren in Green Bay, took over at quarterback. With running back Shaun Alexander and a pair of talented

receivers—Koren Robinson and Darrell Jackson—waiting for him downfield, Hasselbeck led the team to a 10–6 record, including a franchise-first 8–0 home mark. One of the most memorable wins came on September 21 against the division-rival St. Louis Rams. Alexander missed the first quarter to be with his wife during the birth of their first daughter, then sped to the stadium with a police escort to help his teammates eke out a 24–23 victory.

In the first round of the playoffs on a frigid January day at Green Bay's Lambeau Field, the two teams battled back and forth to end regulation play at 27–27. When the Seahawks won the coin toss before overtime began, Hasselbeck confidently said, "We want the ball, and we're gonna score"—a statement picked up by the referee's microphone and

MATT HASSELBECK WAS PERHAPS OVERCONFIDENT OF A PLAYOFF WIN IN GREEN BAY

For the Birds

The first thing fans at Seattle's CenturyLink Field see coming out of the tunnel at game time is Taima, an Augur hawk that has become a live mascot for the team. Taima, which means "thunder," leads the Seahawks out of the tunnel before every home game. Then the bird, which weighs about three pounds and has a four-and-a-half-foot wingspan, swoops across the field at speeds of up to 100 miles per hour before meeting up with its trainer, David Knutson, on the sidelines. Taima, who was hatched on April 21, 2005, at the World Bird Sanctuary in St. Louis, Missouri, started flying through the 67,000-seat stadium at the start of the 2005 season when the bird was just 5 months old. Fans and players quickly developed a bond with the graceful hawk. Knutson spends as much time as he can during the games roaming the sidelines with Taima on his hand, stopping to let spectators stroke the bird and say hello. "It's almost become like a buddha, where people rub his belly for good luck," Knutson said. "The fans love that bird."

LINEBACKER CHAD BROWN WAS A TACKLING THREAT IN THE EARLY 2000s

broadcast across the stadium and on television. The quarterback wished he could have eaten his words when, just a few plays later, he launched a pass that was intercepted and returned for a touchdown and a 33–27 Green Bay victory.

With the offense firing on all cylinders, the Seahawks bulked up defensively in the off-season, adding players such as safety Michael Boulware. Collectively, the defense intercepted 23 passes, sacked opposing quarterbacks 36 times, and recovered 20 fumbles in 2004. With Hasselbeck passing for 3,382 yards and Alexander rushing for 1,696 more, the Seahawks returned to the playoffs. Seattle's Wild Card clash against St. Louis came down to the wire. The Rams led 27–20 with less than a minute left to play, but Hasselbeck drove the Seahawks down to the five-yard line. Unfortunately, his fourth-down pass thudded to the ground, and Seattle's season ended short of the Super Bowl once more.

QUARTERBACKS FEARED THE SIGHT OF TACKLE ROCKY BERNARD BARRELING TOWARD THEM

MIKE HOLMGREN DID NOT MINCE WORDS WHEN MAKING HIS OPINIONS KNOWN

Seattle Gets Its Shot

hen the Seahawks started the 2005 season 2–2, many fans predicted that the year would end in disappointment. But Seattle shocked the sports world by putting together a string of 11 straight wins, including a 42–0 shredding of the Philadelphia Eagles. "This year, the ball is bouncing a little bit for us," Holmgren said. "We're getting wins that in years past might have slipped away." One primary reason was the stellar play of the veteran heart of the offensive line: center Robbie Tobeck, left guard Steve Hutchinson, and left tackle Walter Jones.

By season's end, the Seahawks had compiled a 13–3 record. This time, postseason elimination wasn't an option; two decades after its last playoff victory, Seattle defeated both the Washington Redskins and the Carolina Panthers to reach Super Bowl XL, where it faced a red-hot Pittsburgh Steelers team. The game was close until the Steelers scored a touchdown in the fourth quarter to go up 21–10 and then fended off the Seahawks for the win.

LINEBACKER LOFA TATUPU LED THE NFL IN INTERCEPTIONS RETURNED FOR TOUCHDOWNS (6) IN 2005

Streaking to the Super Bowl

Losing the first game of the 2005 season was not the ideal start for a team that had hopes of making it to the Super Bowl for the first time. By Week 4, the Seahawks owned a mediocre 2–2 record. But after the following week's 37–31 victory over its division rivals, the St. Louis Rams, Seattle just couldn't lose. The team trounced the Houston Texans 42–10 in Week 6 and beat the Dallas Cowboys 13–10 with a last-second field goal in Week 7. After a week off, it topped the Arizona Cardinals 33–19, and then earned another win against the Rams with a mark of 31–16. The winning streak continued for 11 weeks, lasting through the next-to-last game of the season. The Seahawks' unstoppable offense, led by quarterback Matt Hasselbeck and running back Shaun Alexander, put 40 or more points on the board 3 times, including a 42–0 shutout against the Philadelphia Eagles. Seattle lost its final game, 23–17, in Green Bay, but had already clinched a playoff berth. That was all the team needed to reach Super Bowl XL.

SEAHAWKS PLAYERS FELT LIKE HIGH-FIVING DURING THEIR 2005 STREAK

Many Seahawks fans were upset with the officiating, as several calls at crucial times nullified big plays by Seattle. Several years later, referee Bill Leavy confessed that he had made some mistakes. "I kicked two calls in the fourth quarter, and I impacted the game," he said. "And as an official, you never want to do that." Both calls were critical. One was a holding call negating a play that put the ball on the Pittsburgh one-yard line, with the Seahawks trailing by four points. The other was called on Hasselbeck, who was penalized for an illegal low block following an interception, even though he actually made the tackle. The extra 15 yards gave Pittsburgh better field position and helped the Steelers score the touchdown that effectively iced the result.

The loss was disappointing, but the Seahawks were determined to show their

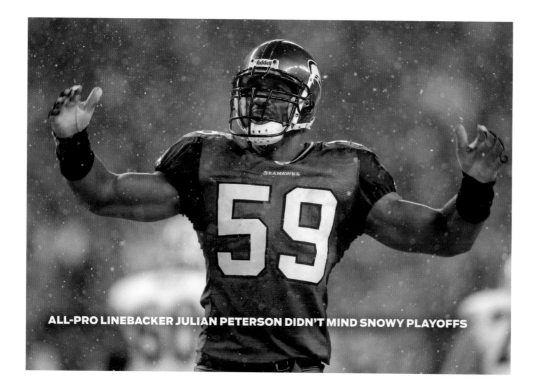

ALL-PRO LINEBACKER JULIAN PETERSON DIDN'T MIND SNOWY PLAYOFFS

resilience as they returned to the playoffs again in 2006. Although the Chicago Bears beat Seattle in a second-round matchup, the Seahawks soared to their fourth consecutive NFC West title in 2007. This time Seattle's postseason ended with a 42–20 playoff drubbing in snowy Green Bay.

That playoff loss seemed to throw the Seahawks off track. They had already lost Hutchinson via free agency, and Tobeck retired after the 2006 season. Fullback Mack Strong, one of the team's best blockers for many years, retired for medical reasons the following year. Jones went down with a catastrophic knee injury in 2008. Hasselbeck struggled with injuries, and the 2008 team started 2–9 before finishing far from postseason contention in Coach Holmgren's final season in Seattle.

fter Seattle went 5–11 in 2009, new coach Jim Mora was fired and replaced by successful University of Southern California coach Pete Carroll. Carroll and new general manager John Schneider went to work shaking up the roster, making more than 100 moves before and during the 2010 season. These moves included trading for bruising running back Marshawn Lynch and drafting hard-hitting safeties Earl Thomas and Kam Chancellor.

The 2010 Seahawks attracted considerable national ridicule by qualifying for the playoffs as division champions, even though they assembled a mere 7–9 regular-season mark. But the team then silenced its critics by defeating the defending Super Bowl champion New Orleans Saints in the opening round of the

The Beastquake

Defying critics who said they had no business hosting a playoff game with their 7–9 record, the 2010 Seahawks clung to a 34–30 lead over the New Orleans Saints with 3:38 remaining. With the ball on Seattle's 33-yard line, quarterback Matt Hasselbeck handed off to Marshawn Lynch, who calls himself "The Beast." Lynch was in full beast mode as he powered through a narrow hole in the line. He then burst into the Saints' secondary, where he shrugged off several tacklers. He stiff-armed cornerback Tracy Porter and broke two final efforts to bring him down—in all, the Saints missed eight tackle attempts—and tumbled backward into the end zone. The run literally set off a minor earthquake; a nearby monitoring station registered seismic activity that lasted for more than a minute from fans stomping their feet. Lynch's run proved critical. The Saints scored a touchdown to narrow the margin, but Seattle then recovered the ensuing onside kick and ran out the clock. "I don't know about you, but my mouth is still agape following Marshawn Lynch's improbable 67-yard touchdown run to seal the Seahawks' unlikely upset of the defending champs," noted ESPN writer Melissa Jacobs.

MARSHAWN LYNCH'S 67-YARD TOUCHDOWN CAME IN HIS FIRST CAREER PLAYOFF GAME

RUNNING BACK JULIUS JONES PLOWED PAST DEFENDERS FOR THREE PARTIAL SEASONS

THE ACROBATIC DOUG BALDWIN EXCHANGED JERSEY NUMBER 15 FOR 89 IN 2012

playoffs, 41–36. "We did it with our crowd and we fit together so beautifully," Carroll said. "We kind of expected to win. I know that sounds crazy, but we did expect to win."

After the Seahawks fell to the Bears a week later, team officials decided that rebuilding the offensive line was the top priority. They selected tackle James Carpenter in the first round of the 2011 NFL Draft and guard John Moffitt in the third. The duo joined the Seahawks' top draft choice from the previous year, tackle Russell Okung. Unfortunately, the group suffered numerous injuries in 2011, and the Seahawks played most of the season with a patchwork offensive line. The result was another 7–9 mark. But more young talent emerged, such as rookie receiver Doug Baldwin, who led the team in catches (51) and yardage (788). San Francisco 49ers coach Jim Harbaugh, who had coached Baldwin at Stanford University and now had to face him twice a year, said ruefully, "Well, I should have drafted him. Yeah, I'm kicking myself for not doing that."

Matt Hasselbeck

QUARTERBACK / SEAHAWKS SEASONS: 2001–10 / HEIGHT: 6-FOOT-4 / WEIGHT: 223 POUNDS

It was Matt Hasselbeck's misfortune to be drafted by the Green Bay Packers. For two seasons, he served as a backup to Brett Favre, who held the NFL record for most consecutive games started, and threw a grand total of only 29 passes. In March 2001, Hasselbeck was traded to the Seattle Seahawks and given the opportunity to step into the starter's role. Hasselbeck was ready. He passed for more than 2,000 yards and 7 touchdowns in 2001. Those numbers increased each season, as he threw 24 touchdowns in Seattle's Super Bowl season in 2005 and had a career-high 28 in 2007. Hasselbeck was injured twice in the 2006 season—first when a linebacker rolled over his right leg, then when he broke several fingers on his left (non-throwing) hand. Still, the gutsy quarterback led the Seahawks to the playoffs in both 2006 and 2007. In 2008, offensive coordinator Gil Haskell called him "the best player on our team." Nevertheless, when Hasselbeck became a free agent after the 2010 season, the team decided not to try to re-sign him, and he quickly joined the Tennessee Titans.

RUSSELL WILSON THREW FOR 3,118 YARDS IN HIS DEBUT 2012 SEASON

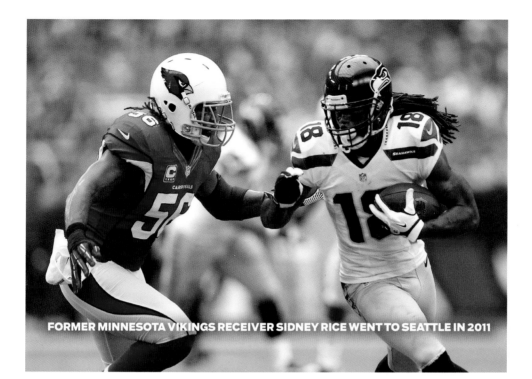

FORMER MINNESOTA VIKINGS RECEIVER SIDNEY RICE WENT TO SEATTLE IN 2011

Seahawks management took considerable heat for its choices in the 2012 NFL Draft. According to experts, the team had "wasted" a third-round pick on Wisconsin quarterback Russell Wilson. However, Wilson proved those experts wrong, showing that his 5-foot-10 stature wasn't a handicap by becoming Seattle's starter. Bobby Wagner, taken a round ahead of Wilson, had a superlative season at middle linebacker and was runner-up for Defensive Rookie of the Year honors. Even the choice of J. R. Sweezy, a defensive end drafted in the seventh round, proved to have been inspired. Sweezy became a part-time starter—at offensive guard, a position he had never played before.

Still, it took a while for all the parts to come together, as Seattle struggled in close contests. When Carroll opened up the playbook for Wilson, who was as adept at scrambling for big yardage as he was at passing, the Seahawks went on an offensive binge at season's end, finishing 11–5. Seattle blew past Washington in the first round of the playoffs and seemed on the verge of one of the greatest postseason comebacks in NFL history the following week at Atlanta. Down 27–7 at the start of the fourth quarter, Seattle took a 28–27 lead with 31 seconds remaining. Unfortunately for the Seahawks, the Falcons had just enough time to kick a game-winning field goal.

While Seattle fans were stunned by the setback, they can only be optimistic. Today's young, rebuilt Seahawks roster is excited about the future. Although Seattle has come close to Super Bowl glory only once in its history, that near miss has only made the Seahawks and their raucous fans more determined to win it all. And should the Seahawks come out on top some Super Bowl Sunday, no matter what the rest of the country might expect, rain probably won't stop their parade.

INDEX